Find Us Faithful

22 ARRANGEMENTS FOR MALE VOICES
BY JOSEPH LINN

11 Two-part Arrangements
11 Four-part Arrangements

Lillenas PUBLISHING COMPANY

KANSAS CITY, MO 64141

Contents

Let There Be Praise

(TB with opt. Trio)

D. T. and M. T.

DICK and MELODIE TUNNEY
Arr. by Doug Holck
TB arr. by Joseph Linn

Let there be praise, let there be joy in our hearts.

1. Sing to the Lord, give Him the
2. For - ev - er - more let His love

(Sing cue notes 2nd time)

glo - ry._____ fill the air,___ and let there___

_____ be praise._____ He in - hab-its the praise___ of His peo -

- ple, and dwells deep with - in._____ The

Je - sus Christ ___ is King.

Let there ___ be praise, let ___ there be joy in ___ our

hearts.

(Sing cue notes 2nd time)

Sing to ___ the ___ Lord, give ___ Him the

For - ev - er - more let ___ His love

In our weak-ness His strength will de - fend _____ us, when His

praise is on _____ our _____ tongue.   So lift your voic - es, _____

Lift your voic - es, _____ sing; _____
_____ with glad - ness sing;   Pro - claim through

all the earth that Je - sus Christ___ is King! And

let there___ be praise, let___ there be joy in___ our

hearts. Sing to___ the___ Lord, give___ Him the

Forever-more let___ His love fill the air,

Let there be praise, be praise,

and let there___ be praise.___

*Left hand optional for these two measures.

And Can It Be?
(TTBB)

CHARLES WESLEY

THOMAS CAMPBELL
Arr. by Joseph Linn

A - maz - ing love! How can it be That Thou, my God, shouldst die for me? He left His Fa - ther's

23

proach the e - ter - nal throne And claim

the crown, through Christ my own. A -

maz - ing love! How can it, can it be

A - maz - ing love! How can it be

A - maz - ing love! How can it, can it be That

Thou, ___ my God, that Thou, my God,

shouldst ___ die ___ for me? ___ A - maz - ing

love! A - maz - ing ___ love!
love! A - maz - ing ___ love! How can it

Up and Away Medley

(TTBB)

Arr. by Joseph Linn

** ♩ = 118   *"Goodby, World, Goodby" (Lister)

I've told all my trou - bles good - by; Good-

by to each tear and each sigh.   This world where I roam can -

**Recording contains 4 extra measures of introduction.

Good-by, world, good - by. Now, don't you weep for me when I'm

gone, 'Cause I won't have to leave here a - lone; And

when I hear that last trum-pet sound, My feet won't stay on the

ground.   Gon-na   rise   with a   shout,   gon-na   fly; _____   Gon-na

ride   with my   Lord   through the   sky. _____   Heav - en   is near,   and

I   can't   stay here.   Good-by,   world,   good - by,   good - by.

Good - by,   world,   good - by,

good - by.

F *"Moving Up to Gloryland" (Abernathy)

♩ = 132

36

mov-in' up to glo - ry, all_____ the way to glo - ry, Mov-in' up to glo - ry -

glo - ry -

land._____

land,_____ glo - ry - land.

*"I'll Fly Away" (Brumley)

Just a few more wea - ry days and then _____

He Giveth More Grace
(TB)

ANNIE JOHNSON FLINT

HUBERT MITCHELL
Arr. by Doug Holck
TB arr. by Joseph Linn

He giv - eth more grace when the bur - dens grow

great - er; He send - eth more strength when the la - bors in -

giv - eth a - gain. When we have ex - haust - ed our

store of en - dur - ance, When our strength has failed ere the

day is half done, When we reach the end of our

hoard - ed re - sourc - es, Our Fa - ther's full___ giv - ing is on - ly be -

gun. For His love has no lim - it; His grace has no mea - sure; His

pow'r has no bound - a - ry known un - to men. For___ out of His

44

Majesty
(TTBB)

J. W. H.

JACK W. HAYFORD
Arr. by Joseph Linn

Maj - es - ty,_____ wor - ship His maj - es - ty;_____

Maj - es - ty, wor-ship His maj - es - ty;____

Maj - es - ty,____

Je - sus, who died, now glo - ri - fied, King of all kings.____

So ex - alt, lift up on high the name____ of

50

Wonderful Savior

(TB, opt. TTBB)

J. D. S.

J. D. SUMNER
Arr. by Joseph Linn

I have start-ed out to fol-low Je - sus. Ev-'ry day, ev-'ry hour I want to be_____ Just a lit-tle more like my bless-ed Je - sus; He means more than all the world___ to

52

The Trees of the Field

(TB)

STEFFI GEISER RUBIN
Based on Isaiah 55:12

STUART DAUERMANN
Arr. by Joseph Linn
Piano transcription by Steve Jones

56

trees of the field will clap their hands,_____ The

trees of the field will clap their hands._____ The

trees of the field will clap their hands_____ While you go

The Love of God
(TTBB)

F. M. L.

F. M. LEHMAN
Arr. by Doug Holck
TTBB arr. by Joseph Linn

O love of God, _____ how rich and pure; _____ How mea-sure-

less _____ and ____ strong! It shall for - ev - er-more en -

dure _____ The saints' and an - gels' song.

62

64

Heavenly Journey Medley

(TTBB)

Arr. by Joseph Linn

*"I'm Climbing Up the Mountain" (Lister)

Once I trav-eled in the val-ley so____ low, so____ low,____ And lone-ly and

die. _____ I'm climb-ing up the moun-tain, climb-ing

high - er up the moun-tain, And I'll reach the oth-er

side by and by, by and by, by and

70

He Hideth My Soul

(TTBB, a capella)

FANNY J. CROSBY

WILLIAM J. KIRKPATRICK
Arr. by Joseph Linn

Je - sus, my Lord, A won-der-ful Sav-ior to me.

Oo_____ cleft of the rock,

He hid - eth my soul in the cleft of the rock, Where

Oo_____ oo____ see,___ I see.___ When___

riv - ers of plea - sure I see._____

clothed in His bright-ness, trans - port-ed, I___ rise To

meet Him in clouds of the sky,_____ His

His___

per - fect sal - va - tion, His won - der-ful___ love___ I'll

Romans 8:28

(TB)

SHIRLEY CANTRELL
Arr. by Joseph Linn

S. C.

All things work to-geth-er for good_____ to them that love the Lord,_

_____ Who are called ac-cord-ing to His pur-pose, my friend;_ It's

writ - ten   in ___ His   Word.   In the   book   of   Ro -mans,   eight___

___ twen-ty - eight,   To the   Church the A -pos-tle   Paul___ did   state___   That

all   things work   to - geth-er for good___   to   them   that   love   the Lord. ___

78

There are man-y prom-is-es in God's Word;— Just to hear them thrills—— my soul. They were all writ-ten there just for me;—— I have no doubt——that it's so.———— But if there

Sa-tan may__ rob me of my hap-pi-ness, But he can't take a-way__ my joy;

'Cause joy is the fruit of the Spir-it in me.__ That's some-thing that he can't de-

stroy. So when it seems that ev-'ry-thing in my life __ has gone wrong, I can

still wear a smile___ and I can still sing a song_____ That all things work to-

geth-er for good_____ to them that love the Lord._____

All things work to - geth-er for good_____ to them that love the Lord._

Who are called ac-cord-ing to His pur-pose, my friend; ___ It's

writ-ten in ___ His Word. In the book of Ro-mans, eight___

___twen-ty eight, To the Church the A-pos-tle Paul did state___ That

all things work to-geth-er for good _____ to them that love the Lord.

_____ All things work to - geth-er for good_____ to

them that love the Lord._____

Find Us Faithful
(TTBB)

J. M.

JON MOHR
Arr. by Joseph Linn

We're pil-grims on the jour - ney of the nar - row road, _____ And

those who've gone be-fore___ us line the way.   Cheer-ing on___ the faith-

- ful,   en - cour-ag-ing___ the wea - ry,   Their   lives a stir-ring test - a-ment___ to

God's sus-tain-ing___   grace.   Sur - round-ed by so great___ a cloud of

wit - ness - es, _____ Let us run the race _____ not on - ly for the

prize; But as those who've gone be-fore _____ us, let us leave to those be-hind

_____ us The her - i - tage _____ of faith-ful-ness _____ passed on through god - ly

lead them to be - lieve, And the lives we live in - spire them to o -

bey. _____ Oh, may all who come be-hind ___ us find us faith - ful.

After all our hopes and dreams have come and gone,_____ And our

chil - dren sift thro' all_____ we've left be - hind,_____ May the

clues that they dis - cov - er and the mem-'ries they un-cov - er Be -

faith - ful; May the fire of our de-vo - tion light their___

way. May the foot - prints that we leave

lead them to be - lieve, And the lives we live in-spire them to o-

Come Before Him
(TTBB)

D. T. and M. T.

DICK and MELODIE TUNNEY
Arr. by Joseph Linn
Piano transcription by Steve Jones

Come be - fore _____ Him, come be -

fore _____ Him! Come un - to Him ___ and

wor - ship Him—— with high - est praise. Come be -

fore—————————— Him, come be - fore——————

Him! Give hon - or to—— His name for - ev - er

Savior,____ De - liv - er - er,____ Je - ho - vah____ God._____ Come be - fore____ Him, come be - fore_____ Him! Come

un - to Him___ and wor - ship Him___ with high - est

praise. Come be - fore_____ Him, come be -

fore Him! Give hon - or to___ His name for - ev - er -

His Love
(TB)

M. C. R.

MARY CAROLYN ROBBINS
Arr. by Dick Bolks
TB arr. by Joseph Linn

God's love reached out to me_____ one day on Cal - va - ry, When I was lost in sin and_____ shame. He par - doned

all my sin,_____ and now He lives with-in; Oh,

bless - ed love of God,_____ so rich and free!_____

_____ His love is broad - er_____ than an - y

As - sured His love
As - sured His love, His love doth sat - is -

fy!   O sin - ner, heed His call;

make Him your All in All.   No tru - er

106

I'm Feeling Fine

(TTBB)

MOSIE LISTER
Arr. by Joseph Linn

soul, 'Cause I knew____ my Lord had con - trol.____ Well, I

knew I was walk-ing in the light, 'Cause I'd been on my knees in the night;

And I'd prayed__ till the Lord__ gave a sign; And now I'm feel-in' might-y

fine.

Feel-in' might-y fine,   yes,____ I'm feel-in' fine;
Well, I'm   feel-in'____ might - y   fine;____   I've got

Heav-en on my mind,   heav - en on my mind.   Don't you know,   yes,____
heav-en____ on   my   mind.____   Don't you   know,____ I want to

____ I want to go   Milk   and   hon - ey, milk____ and hon-ey flow.
go   Where   the   milk____ and hon-ey   flow.____   There's a

Light that al-ways shines, light____ that al-ways shines In this heart of mine, in____
light____ that al-ways shines____ Down in - side____ this heart of

____this heart of mine. Heav-en, heav - en on my, heav-en on my mind; And
mine.____ I've got heav-en, heav - en on my mind;

now I'm feel-in' might-y fine.

I've been walk-in' with Je-sus all the time;

We're walk-in' and talk-in' as we climb._____ We're trav'ling a road to the

114

116

Ten Thousand Angels
(TB)

R. O.

RAY OVERHOLT
Arr. by Tom Fettke
TB arr. by Joseph Linn

Heavenly Love Medley

(TTBB)

Arr. by Joseph Linn

*"Heavenly Love" (Ellis)

Heav-en-ly love_____ was all that could help me;_____ I was a-

stray,_____ so sad and a - lone.   I looked a - bove,_____ my bur-dens all

*"When God Dips His Love in My Heart" (Derricks)

133

All That Thrills My Soul

(TTBB)

T. H.

THORO HARRIS
Arr. by Joseph Linn
Piano transcription by Steve Jones

Lyrics:

Who can cheer the heart like Je - sus,
By His pres-ence all di - vine?
True and ten-der, pure and pre - cious,
Oh, how blest to call Him mine!

By the crys-tal flow-ing riv - er With the ran-somed I will

sing, And for-ev - er___ and for - ev - er

Praise and glo - ri - fy the King. All___ that thrills my soul is

140

The Wonder of It All

(TB)

G. B. S.

GEORGE BEVERLY SHEA
Arr. by Doug Holck
TB arr. by Joseph Linn

1. There's the won - der of
won - der of

With warmth ♩ = ca. 88

sun - set at eve - ning;_____ The won - der as sun - rise I
spring-time and har - vest;_____ The sky,____ the stars,____ the

cresc. little by little

see._____ But the won - der of won - ders that____
sun._____ But the won - der of won - ders that____

mel. cresc. little by little

cresc. little by little

me.＿＿＿＿＿＿＿ Oh, the won - der of it all, the

won - der of it all, Just to think that God＿＿ loves

me.＿＿＿＿＿＿＿ 2. There's the

all, the won - der of it all, Just to think that God____ loves

me._____ Just to think that God____ loves__ me,_____

_____ He loves me._____

A New Name in Glory

(TB)

C. A. M.

C. AUSTIN MILES
Arr. by Mosie Lister
TB arr. by Joseph Linn

I was once a sin-ner, but I came Par-don to re-ceive from my Lord._____ This was free-ly giv-en, and I found That He al-ways kept His word. There's a new name writ-ten down in

Fear-ing naught but God's an - gry frown,_____ When the heav-ens o - pened

and I saw That my name was writ-ten down, writ-ten down. There's a

new name writ-ten down in glo-ry; And it's mine,_____ oh, yes, it's

mine. And the white-robed an-gels sing the sto-ry,_____ "A sin - ner has come

home, has come home." There's a new name writ-ten down in

glo - ry; And it's mine,_____ oh, yes, it's mine. With my

sins for-giv-en I am bound for heav-en, Nev - er-more to roam. With my

sins for - giv-en I am bound for heav - en, Nev - er -

more to roam, no more to roam.

Zion's Hill
(TB)

J. A. C.

JAMES A. CRUTCHFIELD
Arr. by Joseph Linn
Piano transcription by Steve Jones

There waits for me a glad to-mor-row,_____ Where
gates of pearl swing o-pen wide; And when I've passed this vale of

sor - row, _____ I'll dwell up - on the oth - er side. Some -

day, be-yond the reach of mor-tal ken; Some - day, God on - ly knows just

where and when— The wheels of mor-tal life shall all stand still, And

mend-ed, _____ And I shall sigh and weep no more. Some -

I shall go to dwell, How I long to dwell,

I shall go to dwell on Zi - on's hill.

Praise God, from Whom All Blessings Flow

(TB, opt. TTBB; a capella)

THOMAS KEN

Melody from *Geistliche Kirchengesäng*, 1623
Arr. by Joseph Linn